BULGARIA

MAJOR WORLD NATIONS

BULGARIA

Julian Popescu

CHELSEA HOUSE PUBLISHERS
Philadelphia

Chelsea House Publishers

Copyright © 2000 by Chelsea House Publishers,
a division of Main Line Book Co.
All rights reserved.
Printed in Malaysia

First Printing.

1 3 5 7 9 8 6 4 2

Library of Congress Cataloging-in-Publication Data

Popescu, Julian.
Bulgaria / Julian Popescu
p. cm. — (Major world nations)
Includes index.
Summary: Surveys the history, topography, government, people,
and culture of Bulgaria
ISBN 0-7910-5380-6 (hc)
1. Bulgaria—Juvenile literature. [1. Bulgaria.] I. Title.
II. Series.
DR67.7.P67 1999
949.9—dc21   99-19239
CIP

ACKNOWLEDGEMENTS

The Author and Publishers are grateful to the following organizations and individuals
for permission to reproduce copyright illustrations in this book:
The Bulgarian Tourist Office; The Mansell Collection Ltd; Novosti Press Agency; Travel
Photo International; D. C. Williamson—London.

CONTENTS

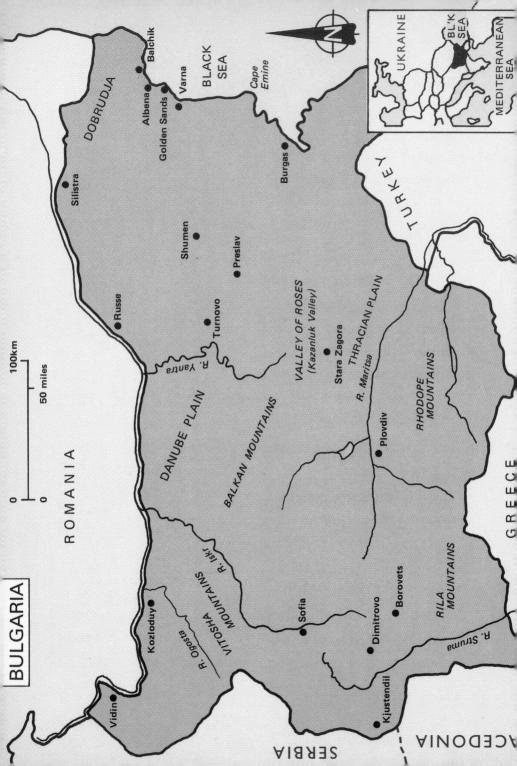

FACTS AT A GLANCE

Land and People

Official Name	Republic of Bulgaria
Location	Southeastern Europe on the Balkan Peninsula
Area	42,835 square miles (110, 987 square kilometers)
Climate	Temperate
Capital	Sofia
Other Cities	Plovdiv, Varna, Ruse
Population	8,810, 000
Population Distribution	Two-thirds urban
Major Rivers	Danube, Iskr, Ogosto, Yantra, Maritsa
Major Lakes	Black Sea
Mountains	Balkans, Vitosha, Central, Rila, Pirin
Highest Point	Mount Mussala (9,597 feet/2,925 meters)
Official Language	Bulgarian
Ethnic Groups	Turkish (8.5 percent); Gypsies (2.5 percent)

Religions	Eastern Orthodox Christian, Muslim
Literacy Rate	98 percent
Average Life Expectancy	Male: 69 years; female: 76 years

Economy

Natural Resources	Timber, copper , roses
Agricultural Products	Tobacco, roses, wheat barley, sugar beets, potatoes
Industries	Chemical, electronics machinery
Major Exports	Tobacco, oil of roses, machinery and equipment
Major Trading Partners	Russia, Germany
Currency	Leva

Government

Form of Government	Parliamentary Republic
Government Bodies	National Assembly (parliament); Council of Ministers
Formal Head of State	President
Voting Rights	All Bulgarians over the age of 18

HISTORY AT A GLANCE

4000 B.C.   Thracians settle in the area now called the Thracian Plain during the Bronze Age. (Archaeological finds show that they made ornaments and idols of bone and marble, and believed in life after death.)

600-500 B.C.   Greek traders establish ports on the Black Sea coast, one of which is Odessos. (Odessos is the present-day city of Varna.)

4th century B.C.   Alexander the Great conquers the entire Balkan area.

2nd century B.C.   Romans establish a province in the area then called Moesea, between the Danube River and the Balkan Mountains. They build new roads and cities.

100 B.C.   Roman Emperor Trajan builds a fort at the site of present day Sofia.

681 A.D.   Bulgars (of Turkic origin) cross the Danube and establish the First Bulgarian Kingdom. This kingdom would last until 1081.

865 A.D.   Tsar Boris I of Bulgaria adopts Christianity as his country's religion and encourages the teaching of the new religion and a new alphabet to all the people.

1014   Tsar Samuel is defeated by the Byzantine emperor Basil II and Bulgaria becomes part of the Byzantine Empire.

1185   Tsar Ivan Assen proclaims the land of Bulgaria to be the Second Bulgarian Kingdom. His reign ends tragically when he is murdered by a nobleman.

1218-1241   Ivan Assen II becomes tsar. Considered one of Bulgaria's greatest rulers, the country prospers under his reign.

1352   Ottoman Turks begin their invasion of the Balkan Peninsula. There is widespread destruction of Bulgarian villages and much fierce fighting. After nine years Bulgaria's tsar surrenders to the Turks and declares himself a vassal of the Turkish sultan. Ottoman rule of the area lasts for five centuries.

1600s   The Turkish Ottoman Empire reaches the peak of its power and control in Bulgaria and the surrounding territories.

1700s   Paussi, a monk from the monastery on Mount Athos, leads the Bulgarian National Revival, attempting to awaken the Bulgarians' desire for freedom from Turkish rule.

1768-1791   A number of wars are waged between the Russian Empire and the Ottoman Empire. The Turks are weakened and forced to give up the territory north of the Danube. Tsarist Russia becomes the champion of the Bulgarian people.

1828-1829	Bulgarians fight with the Russians in another war against the Turks in which neighboring Greece finally gains its independence from the Ottoman Empire.
1876	The Bulgarians, led by a poet Hristo Botev, rise up against the Turkish rule. The Turks fight back with cruelty, enraging much of Europe.
1877	Russia declares war on Turkey in order to help the struggling Bulgarians.
1878	After the war, a European congress is convened which decides to divide Bulgaria into three parts: the north is made an independent principality; the south is made independent on domestic matters but remains under the rule of the Turkish sultan; Thrace and Macedonia are still under Turkish rule.
1879	Turnovo constitution is written for the new Bulgarian state.
1908	After years of struggle to be an independent country, Bulgarians decide they will officially be a monarchy and Ferdinand is made the first king.
1914	The First World War begins in the Balkans with the murder of Archduke Ferdinand of Austria. Bulgaria sides with Germany in the fight against the Western powers and Russia.
1919	King Ferdinand abdicates the throne in favor of his son, Boris III.
1923-1924	Revolutionary workers led by the communists riot, trying to seize power. The revolution is eventually crushed.
1941	Bulgaria becomes an ally of Germany in World

11

War II, declaring war on the United States and Britain but refusing to join in the war against its neighbor, the Soviet Union.

1944 Soviet army invades Bulgaria after their defeat of the Germans.

1946 King Simeon II of Bulgaria is deposed by the communist element, and the country is declared a People's Republic. George Dimitrov becomes its leader.

1954 Bulgaria joins the Warsaw Pact and becomes one of the Soviet Union's most faithful allies. Todor Zhivhov becomes the leader of Bulgaria and will remain its leader until the overthrow of communism in 1989.

1954-1989 The communist government bans all political opposition, free speech, and travel abroad.

1989 Communist leader Todor Zhivkov and his government are overthrown and Bulgaria embarks as a parliamentary republic. Many Bulgarians return to their former traditions and religions which had been suppressed during the communist reign.

1989-1996 The Bulgarian government changes hands seven times amidst the great economic and political upheaval following the overthrow of communism. The change to a democratic government and free-market economy does not go smoothly.

1997 The people of Bulgaria rise up in protest of the corrupt government, rampant unemployment, inflation, and starvation. They demand new elections and the current government steps down after the strikes and protests paralyze the country for over a month.

1

Land of Mountains

Bulgaria is part of the Balkan Peninsula, one of Europe's three great southern peninsulas. "Balkan" is a Turkish word meaning mountain. Other European countries which belong to the Balkans are Greece, Albania, Romania and Yugoslavia.

Bulgaria means "land of the Bulgars." The country is divided by the Balkan Mountains into two halves: north and south. To the north of the mountains, a fertile plain and steppes, bordered by the Danube River and the Black Sea, stretch away to the horizon. This rich farmland produces most of Bulgaria's wheat and barley.

To the south of the Balkan Mountains lies the Thracian Plain, in the basin of the Maritsa River. Further south still are the massive ranges of the Rila and Rhodope Mountains, broken up by plateaux and gorges and fast-flowing rivers. Sheltered on three sides by mountains, the Thracian Plain is also called Bulgaria's Garden. Flowers grow in great numbers here, and vines, tobacco, fruit trees and many vegetables are also cultivated.

In the winter, the Arctic winds from the Russian steppes freeze the rivers and lakes. These winds bring much snow which, to the delight of skiers, covers the mountains and valleys. But spring comes early. The fields change their covering of snow or bare earth to a carpet of green, and flowers can be seen everywhere. The orchards are full of blossoms which fill the air with scent.

Today, Bulgaria is an independent parliamentary republic struggling to reform and implement changes after an era of political and economic upheaval following the overthrow of communism in 1989. With an area of 42,823 square miles (110,912 square kilometers), the country is just under half the size of Great Britain. Its population of nine million is made up of Bulgarians, Turks, Romanians and a few other racial minorities such as Greeks and Macedonians.

The Bulgarians are a hospitable and hard-working people. They belong to the Slav family of peoples and are related to the Russians, Serbs, Czechs, Slovaks and Poles. Unlike their blue-eyed, fair-haired Slav cousins, most Bulgarians have dark faces and black hair. Because they lived for many centuries under Turkish rule, the Bulgarians are now proud of being an independent nation.

The Bulgarians, like the Russians, use the Cyrillic alphabet for writing and reading, instead of the Latin alphabet which we all know. The Cyrillic alphabet is named after St. Cyril, a Bulgarian monk born in Thessalonika in 827 A.D. and nicknamed the Philosopher. Cyril and his brother Methodius spread Christianity among the Slav peoples and taught them to read and write their own alphabet.

A woman with typical Bulgarian features in a market in Sofia. The Bulgarians belong to the Slav family of peoples.

The people buy and sell goods using money called *leva*. The word means "lions" in Bulgarian. There are strict currency regulations and it is illegal to take large amounts of *leva* out of the country.

In 1997, one U.S. dollar equaled about 1,800 *leva*. Although Bulgaria was at war with Great Britain and the United States during the Second World War, the Bulgarians did not fight or send troops to attack the Soviet Union. The government, however,

15

allowed the German armies to pass through their country and fight the Serbs and Greeks. When the Soviets defeated the Germans and came from the East in the summer of 1944, they occupied Bulgaria without firing a shot. So, unlike its neighbors, Bulgaria did not become a battlefield and most of its towns and villages were left undisturbed.

After the war, new factories were built in towns all over Bulgaria. Rivers were dammed for irrigation and for producing hydroelectric power. High-tension cables crossed mountains and valleys like giant cobwebs. Many of the peasants left their villages to become factory workers. The towns expanded with new housing estates, complete with super-stores, gardens and parking garages, being built every year. Roads were widened and improved to cope with increased traffic. New multi-story hotels and swimming pools were built at resorts on the Black Sea coast to cater to tourists who visit the country each year.

Nearly half the population of present-day Bulgaria are peasants and farmers who work long hours in the fields. They can be seen still using wooden pitchforks and rakes for making hay. But the hot sun and fertile soil combine to make Bulgaria a great exporter of vegetables, wines and tobacco and, above all, the scented oil or attar of roses to many countries in Europe.

Many of the mountains are wild and shrouded in mist. Shepherds with their dogs and donkeys move their flocks of sheep from meadow to meadow in spring and summer. When the cold weather starts in the autumn, the men drive their flocks down the mountains to the meadows of the plains.

16

A modern housing development in Sofia, in contrast with the more traditional building in the foreground.

By contrast, in April 1979, the first Bulgarian astronaut, Georgi Ivanov, was launched on board the spacecraft Soyuz 33 on a joint mission with the Soviet Union. He spent two days orbiting in space before returning to earth in Central Siberia. Today, continued economic depression makes life hard on most Bulgarians.

Bulgaria has many splendid mountain slopes which are used for skiing and tobogganing in winter. It also has mountain resorts

17

Georgi Ivanov, the first Bulgarian astronaut (right), with his Soviet colleague, Nikolai Rukavishnikov.

with clear and healthy air, and spas with hot springs. But the country is probably best known for its hundreds of golden beaches on the Black Sea coast. Let us visit this country in the heart of the Balkans and look more closely at the land and way of life of the Bulgarian people.

2

Geography and Climate

Bulgaria lies in the Lower Danube Basin in southeastern Europe. The country has lofty mountain ranges which stretch beyond its borders. These are the Balkan Mountains, or Stara Planina, in the middle of the country which are a continuation of the Carpathian Mountains, and the Rhodope Mountains in the south.

Bulgaria borders on Romania in the north and shares with it a long stretch of the Danube River. Bulgaria's neighbor in the west is Yugoslavia. In the south, the border runs over mountains and hills separating Bulgaria from Greece. Bulgaria's neighbor in the southeast is Turkey. The border here runs across the Thracian Plain. In the east, Bulgaria borders on the Black Sea. Its Black Sea coastline is 235 miles (378 kilometers) long.

The Black Sea, so goes the legend, acquired its name because long ago many fishermen who went to sea were drowned in storms or never returned, so that seaside villages were full of mourning women wearing black veils. The Black Sea was originally a freshwater lake, but today it flows into the Sea of Marmara through the Bosphorus Strait, which belongs to Turkey, and then into the Mediterranean. The Black Sea is tideless and is Bulgaria's most important waterway.

Northern Bulgaria, the land between the Danube and the Balkan Mountains, is called the Danube tableland and consists of fertile black earth. Further east is Dobrudja, a plateau of rolling hills formed of ancient mountains. The climate here is hot and dry in summer. Along the coast there are lagoons and golden beaches surrounded by fir and pine trees.

The main mountain range in Bulgaria, the Balkan Mountains, stretches across the middle of the country from west to east, and ends at Cape Emine on the Black Sea coast. The Balkan Mountains are composed of hard granite and crystalline rocks. They are not very high and are well covered with forests. Mount Botev, the highest peak, rises to 7,796 feet (2,376 meters). There are also valleys and passes, and several main roads have been built through the mountains to link northern and southern Bulgaria.

Just south of this range, near Sofia, the capital, are the Vitosha Mountains. Mount Vitosha, which can be seen from the center of Sofia, rises to 7,513 feet (2,290 meters). The Central Mountains, or Sredna Gora, run parallel to the Vitosha Mountains. The highest peak in this range is Mount Bogdan, which rises to 5,263 feet (1,604 meters). The famous Valley of Roses is found in between these two mountain chains.

The Rila Mountains and the neighboring Pirin Mountains are in the southwest of the country. The mountains consist mainly of

The Vitosha Mountains, near Sofia—popular with winter sports lovers.

granite and limestone. Their ridges are pointed, bare and rocky. Snow patches linger on their upper slopes until late in July. The highest peak in the entire Balkan Peninsula is found here. Mount Mussala in the Rila Mountains rises to 9,597 feet (2,925 meters)— just three feet (one meter) higher than Mount Olympus in Greece. There is a story that when the Greeks heard that Mount Mussala was higher than their own Olympus, they piled stones on its peak to make it higher but the strong winds sent them tumbling down again. The highest peak in the Pirin Mountains is Mount Vikhren which rises to 9,564 feet (2,915 meters).

The Rhodope Mountains lie to the east. These mountains are famous for their beautiful scenery. Rain and wind have worn deep

21

Skiers in the Vitosha Mountains.

gorges through which fast-flowing rivers rush over boulders and broken rock. The highest peak in the Rhodope range is Mount Golyan Perelik rising to 7,192 feet (2,192 meters).

The Belasitsa Mountains are situated in the country's southwestern corner and they are shared with Yugoslavia. The highest peak here is Mount Radomir, which rises to 6,657 feet (2,029 meters).

Nearly 30 percent of Bulgaria's territory is made up of mountains. Thick forests of pine and fir trees, as well as hornbeam, silver birch and beech trees cover the hills and mountain slopes. The valleys have many acacia and poplar trees. Higher up the mountains, the trees give way to stunted pines and alpine meadows. Hardy star-shaped flowers grow in patches among the grey and brown rocks. Some are bright blue and yellow; others pink and white. Gentians, saxifrage and edelweiss grow here among lichens and mosses. Giant ferns mixed with nettles and cow-parsley grow in forest clearings and among the trees.

The mountains and hills are also the home of many species of wild birds and animals. Nutcrackers and stone pipits can be seen in many places as well as the crested crow and black woodpecker. The brown bear has his den among the rocks, while the wild boar and red stag roam the forests. The bears are reputed to be friendly but the wild boar can be dangerous. Red squirrels and foxes, wild cats and elks live in the hills and valleys. Wolves sometimes attack flocks of sheep grazing the alpine pastures. For this reason, the sheep have bells round their necks and each flock is guarded night and day by shepherds armed with cudgels, and their dogs.

Bulgaria's plains account for nearly one third of its territory. The northern plain on the banks of the Danube produces good crops of wheat, barley, maize and sugar beet. The Dobrudja in the northeast is also called Bulgaria's granary, for here large quantities of wheat are harvested as early as June.

The Thracian Plain, which is flat as a pancake and lies in the southern half of the country, is famous for its tobacco plantations, orchards and vineyards. The Maritsa River, known in ancient times as the Hebrus, flows through the middle of the plain and provides farmers with water for irrigation. Acacia trees, poplars, limes and willows are found almost everywhere in the plain. Foxes and hares find hiding-places there. Common birds are pheasants and bustards.

Bulgaria is situated between the latitudes of 41 and 44 degrees North. This means that its climate belongs to the moderate continental zone, being influenced by both the Mediterranean and Black Seas. Most of the rain falls in the spring, June being the wettest month. The Dobrudja in the northeast of the country is

The Vača River, which flows through the Rhodope Mountains.

Sandstone rock formations in the Pirin Mountains.

the driest area, with an annual average rainfall of 18 inches (450 millimeters). The rainfall in the mountains is much heavier, with an annual average of 47 inches (1,200 millimeters). The summers are hot and have plenty of sunshine, but the winters are cold especially in the mountains. The Thracian Plain boasts a mild Mediterranean climate. The mean July temperature of the country as a whole varies between 72 and 75 degrees Fahrenheit (22 and 24 degrees Celsius). By contrast, the coldest month of the year is January when the mean temperature varies between 32 and 29 degrees Fahrenheit (0 and minus 2 degrees Celsius).

3

The Lower Danube Basin

Bulgaria's most important river and navigable waterway is the Danube, which drains all the rivers from the northern slopes of the Balkan Mountains. The Danube also drains all rivers from the southern slopes of the Carpathian Mountains in neighboring Romania. This drainage area is called the Lower Danube Basin.

In its lower reaches, the Danube flows sluggishly. The Bulgarian and Romanian banks here are more than half a mile (over a kilometer) apart. There are islands full of swamps and reeds where storks and herons nest. Some of the islands belong to Bulgaria while others belong to Romania. Otherwise the border between the two countries runs along the middle of the river over a length of 292 miles (471 kilometers). The most important Bulgarian tributaries of the Danube are the Iskr, Ogosta and Yantra rivers which rise in the Balkan Mountains. The Iskr is 228 miles (368 kilometers) long, the Yantra, 177 miles (285 kilometers) and the Ogosta, only 89 miles (144 kilometers). When the snows melt in the mountains in spring these rivers bring down mud and silt, and deposit them in the Danube–hence the need for constant dredging of the river to keep it open for steamers and barges.

The Bulgarian port of Ruse is today linked to the Romanian port of Giurgiu (named after St. George.) by a long railway bridge and a modern bridge for motor traffic called Friendship Bridge. These bridges have to be long not only because the river is wide, but also because of the marshes which have for centuries made communications across the river difficult. Today, Bulgarian international trucks and cars cross this bridge into Romania and then head for Bucharest, the capital of Romania, or for Western countries.

The Lower Danube is now linked to the Black Sea by a 38-mile (61-kilometer) long canal across the Dobrudja on the Romanian side of the border. This canal has made it possible for Bulgarian steamers and ships in the Black Sea to travel faster to the Bulgarian ports on the Danube.

At Ruse, corn, timber and other farming produce are loaded either on river craft to go up the Danube or onto ocean-going boats to sail down the river and the canal into the Black Sea, and from there to the Mediterranean. Traffic on the Danube has become very heavy. There are Russian boats flying the Russian flag and Turkish ships flying the Crescent. There are also boats from Greece and Egypt which call at the ports of Silistra and Ruse to deliver their merchandise.

Many of the people who have homes near the Danube make a living as fishermen, for many types of fish live in the river, including sturgeon, from which caviar, a great delicacy, is taken while the fish is still alive. Another industry of the Danube is the cutting of reeds, for in recent years it has been discovered that these contain cellulose, which is used for making paper and cardboard. The reeds are loaded onto steamers and taken down river to factories to be pulped and the cellulose extracted. Other marshes and swamps on the banks of the Danube have been drained and are now used to grow crops, only the Sreburna Lake being spared as a nature reserve for wildlife.

Bulgaria, together with a number of other countries, belongs to the Danube River Commission which regulates navigation and keeps the river clear of sand and silt. It also helps to keep the river clean, banning industrial pollution which would otherwise kill valuable fish and wildlife.

4

Early History and Tsars

The history of human settlement in Bulgaria goes back a long time. Excavations made at Turnovo have shown that primitive man lived there many thousands of years before the Stone Age. He was a hunter of wild animals, wandering from place to place in search of food. Other excavations have shown that Sofia was first settled some 8,000 years ago; while the city of Plovdiv, in the middle of the Thracian Plain, had a settlement 5,000 years ago. In fact the Thracians who gave their name to the Thracian Plain settled in the Balkans in the Bronze Age some 4,000 years before the birth of Christ. They made ornaments and idols of bone and marble. They were an artistic and civilized people and are known to have believed in life after death. Orpheus, the legendary singer and charmer of antiquity, was a Thracian.

Five or six centuries before the birth of Christ, Greek traders came from the Mediterranean and established ports on the Black Sea coast. One of these ports was Odessos, today known as Varna.

Gold drinking horns, made by the Thracians who settled in the Balkans some 4,000 years before the birth of Christ. These horns are now in Sofia's National Museum of History.

The Greeks traded with the Thracians and grew wealthy. Later, the Thracians took over and ruled the Greek Black Sea cities.

Alexander the Great conquered the whole of the Balkans as far as the Danube during his short reign in the fourth century before Christ. Later still, Roman influence spread to the Balkans in the second century B.C. They established a province between the Danube and the Balkan Mountains called Moesia, and built roads and new cities. In the first century A.D., the Roman Emperor Trajan built a fort at Sofia, which was then called Ulpia Serdica.

Roman colonists settled in the plains and along the coast, and the province prospered.

But Roman rule did not last long. Barbarian horsemen from the north crossed the Danube and forced the Roman garrisons and settlers to withdraw to the safety of Italy. Tribes of Slavs came with these barbarians and settled south of the Danube in the fifth and sixth centuries A.D. The land they settled in belonged to the Byzantine Empire, with its capital at Constantinople.

In the early Middle Ages the Bulgars, who were of Turkic origin and lived in the steppes of the Volga region, migrated to the west. They were ferocious fighters led by Khan (or Overlord)

Pre-Cyrillic writing found in the binding of a book.

Asparuch. They crossed the Danube and defeated the Byzantine army. Khan Asparuch then established the First Bulgarian Kingdom in 681 A.D. This kingdom lasted until 1081 A.D. and consisted of an alliance of Bulgarian and Slav tribes.

The mixture of Bulgarian and Slav peoples gave birth to the new Bulgarian nation as we know it today. They tilled the land and did much to develop the country's resources. Under Khan Krum, who reigned from 802 to 814, the Bulgarian Kingdom grew stronger and expanded. Khan Omurtag, who followed him as leader and reigned until 831, signed an important peace treaty with Byzantium.

Boris I, who styled himself Tsar, will always be remembered because in 865 he adopted Christianity and encouraged the brothers Cyril and Methodius to teach the people their new alphabet and to preach the new religion. In this way, the foundations were laid for the beginning of Slav religion and literature.

A necklace dating from the Second Bulgarian Kingdom (1185-1396).

Tsar Simeon, who followed Tsar Boris I and reigned from 893 to 927, brought writers and scholars to his capital at Preslav. Thus began the golden age of Bulgarian culture, and over two thousand manuscripts have been preserved from those days. Tsar Simeon also built many palaces and churches.

After the death of Tsar Simeon, the influence and power of Byzantium grew again. Tsar Samuel, who came to the throne in 980, waged war against the Byzantines. He was defeated in 1014 by Emperor Basil II, who took 15,000 Bulgarians prisoner and had their eyes put out. Bulgaria then became a province of the Byzantine Empire.

The Second Bulgarian Kingdom was proclaimed in 1185 by Tsar Ivan Assen. He was the first ruler to have a new capital at Turnovo. Tsar Assen's rule came to a tragic end when he was murdered by a nobleman. Tsar Kaloyan came to the throne in 1197 and reigned until 1207. He made Bulgaria a powerful country again by capturing Varna and conquering Thrace and Macedonia in the west. Like Assen, Tsar Kaloyan was murdered by plotters while he was besieging the city of Salonika.

Ivan Assen II, the son of Assen I, was proclaimed Tsar in 1218 and he reigned until 1241. He is considered one of Bulgaria's greatest rulers because under him the country prospered and literature and the arts flourished. After his death, a new period of decline set in and the country suffered much at the hands of Tartar raiders who killed and plundered on their way. By the end of the fourteenth century, Bulgaria was divided into two kingdoms, one with its capital at Turnovo and the other with the new capital at Vidin.

5

Turkish Rule

The Ottoman Turks began the invasion of the Balkan Peninsula in 1352. Their armies plundered Bulgarian villages and towns. At first, fierce battles raged between Bulgarians and Turks in the plains and mountains. The Turks showed no mercy towards Bulgarian prisoners and often had their heads cut off for fun.

The Turkish army advanced across the Thracian Plain and captured Plovdiv in 1362. Nine years later, Bulgaria's last tsar, Ivan Shishman, declared himself the vassal of the Turkish Sultan Murad I and paid tribute. The Turks eventually took Sofia in 1382. They burned down Turnovo in 1393 and captured Vidin three years later. So, in 1396, the Turkish rule of Bulgaria began when a Turkish Governor General, called Beglergeb, was appointed.

Turkish rule lasted for five centuries and has always been regarded as the darkest period in Bulgarian history. The Turks imposed taxes on the population and on farm produce. They recruited young boys between the ages of 11 and 12 for their armies and regarded all Christians as infidels. The Bulgarian peasants were treated as serfs by the Turkish rulers and were not allowed to leave their farms and villages. They were put to work for the Turkish garrisons and forced to repair the roads. The peasants rioted from time to time but the Turkish soldiers soon crushed them, executing the ringleaders in public. However, the Turks also built roads, mosques and baths, and kept law and order; and trade began to grow.

The struggle of the Bulgarian people for national independence began in the 18th century when the whole of the Balkans was under Turkish domination. A monk called Paissi from the monastery on Mount Athos is regarded as the leader of the Bulgarian National Revival. He preached on the long history of the Bulgarian people, awakening their longing for freedom.

During the 18th century, the Ottoman Empire stretched from the

A statue of Paissi, the monk who was largely responsible for inspiring the Bulgarian independence movement.

Mediterranean to the Black Sea and the Crimea. It was one of the largest empires of eastern Europe and it came increasingly into conflict with the Russian Empire. The armies of Empress Catherine the Great of Russia defeated the Turks and conquered the Ukraine with its valuable Black Sea ports. After a war which lasted from 1768 to 1774, a peace treaty was signed at Kainardzhi. But other wars between Russia and Turkey followed in 1787 and 1791. The Ottoman Empire suffered setbacks in these wars, and the Turkish Sultan was forced to give up his claims to land north of the Danube.

At the turn of the 19th century, tsarist Russia had become the champion and defender of the Bulgarian people. Many Bulgarians fled to Russia and there joined the tsarist army. Under their captain Georgi Marmachev, Bulgarians fought with the Russians in the 1828-29 war against Turkey. After this war, Greece was given independence from the Turks.

Russia's successes encouraged the Bulgarian patriots to continue their struggle against Turkish rule. A famous Bulgarian leader of the time was Stefan Karadzha, whose bronze bust can now be seen on a stone plinth in the center of Varna. Hristo Botev was a great poet and revolutionary, who wrote about the struggle of the Bulgarian people for freedom. Vasil Levski was another leader who made preparations for an uprising of the Bulgarian people against the Turks. But he was caught by the Turkish secret police in 1873 and hanged in public.

A general uprising, led by the revolutionary poet Hristo Botev, took place in Bulgaria in 1876. The Turkish troops fought back, killing many people and burning villages. The whole of Europe was angered by the cruelty of the Turks. This gave Tsar Alexander II of

The Monument of the Liberators, an equestrian statue of Tsar Alexander II of Russia with his officers.

Russia his opportunity to come to the aid of the Bulgarian people. Russia declared war on Turkey in 1877 and, with the help of Romanian troops, the Russians crossed the Danube and defeated the Turks led by Osman Pasha at Pleven. In 1878, a treaty was signed at San Stefano, a suburb of Istanbul, giving independence to most of Bulgaria.

The Bulgarians have always been grateful to Tsar Alexander II. They called him the Liberator and built a monument in his honor in one of Sofia's finest squares. The monument is made of bronze and shows Tsar Alexander on horse surrounded by his troops and gun carriages.

The great powers of Europe were not pleased with the treaty

Tsar Ferdinand of Bulgaria, 1908.

between Russia and Turkey so a Congress was held in Berlin in July 1878. The Congress decided to divide Bulgaria into three parts. The north of the country became an independent Bulgarian Principality. The south was made autonomous in domestic matters, but remained under the sovereignty of the Sultan of Turkey. Thrace and Macedonia were returned to Turkey. This division of the country did not last for long. Bulgarian patriots led another rebellion against the Turks and the country was united after a treaty signed in Bucharest in 1885.

A few years later, the Bulgarians decided they wished to become a monarchy. They chose a German prince, Ferdinand of Saxe-Coburg-Gotha, as their king. Prince Ferdinand was crowned Tsar Ferdinand of Bulgaria in 1908.

6

Balkan and World Wars

Ever since the beginning of the 20th century, the statesmen of Europe have called the Balkans a gunpowder keg because the slightest incident there would spark off a war. Bulgaria and its neighbors twice went to war over border disputes before the outbreak of the First World War.

The first Balkan war was waged in 1912 by Serbia and Bulgaria against Turkey over its remaining European possessions. The war ended in defeat for Turkey, which from now on ceased to be a great European power.

The second Balkan war took place in 1913. Bulgaria attacked Greece and Serbia, claiming that Macedonia was part of its territory. Romanian troops then attacked Bulgaria from the north and the war ended quickly in defeat for Bulgaria. A peace treaty was signed in Bucharest in August 1913 which meant that Bulgaria gave up its claims to Macedonia and also lost a strip of land in southern Dobrudja to Romania.

The First World War began in the Balkans in 1914 when the Austro-Hungarian Emperor declared war on Serbia over the mur-

Bulgarian troops on their way to fight against Turkey in the first Balkan war of 1912 in which they were victorious.

der of the Austrian Archduke Franz Ferdinand by a Bosnian student. Bulgaria joined Germany and the Austro-Hungarian Empire against the Western Powers and Russia. Things went badly for Bulgaria in the war. An armistice was signed in Salonika in 1918, as a result of which Bulgaria lost more territory to Greece, Romania and Yugoslavia.

King Ferdinand abdicated in 1919 and his son King Boris III came to the throne. His reign was not easy because in 1923 chaos spread to the country. Revolutionary workers led by the communists rioted and went on the rampage. They wanted to seize power but failed and their revolution was crushed in 1924. In 1940, Hitler's Germany gave Hungary a large part of Transylvania which had previously belonged to Romania. Taking advantage of

40

Romania's problems, the Bulgarian government ordered its troops to invade southern Dobrudja which the country had lost in 1918. A year later, Bulgaria became the ally of Germany and allowed German troops to be stationed in Bulgarian cities. In December 1941, Bulgaria declared war on Britain and the United States but refused to take part in the war against the Soviet Union. King Boris III died suddenly in 1943 in mysterious circumstances and young Prince Simeon came to the throne. He was called King Simeon II and ruled through a Regency Council because he was under age. During his reign, which was to be brief, Sofia and a few other towns were bombed by American planes and life became difficult for the people. When the victorious Soviet army reached the Bulgarian borders in September 1944, the Bulgarian government declared its neutrality. This was not accepted by the Soviet Union, who declared war. The Russian Marshal, Fedor Tolbukhin, ordered his troops to occupy Bulgaria. The Bulgarian Communist Party, which called itself the Fatherland Front, took over the government, and later named a town in Bulgaria after Marshal Tolbukhin.

King Simeon II was deposed on September 15, 1946 by the communist government and the country was declared a People's Republic. The communist leader Georgi Dimitrov came back to Bulgaria from Russia where he had been living and became prime minister. The peace treaty with the victorious powers was signed in 1947 and the Soviet troops left the country. The Bulgarian government nationalized industry and transportation, and the land was distributed to peasant cooperatives. Bulgaria joined the Council for Mutual Economic Aid (Common Market) of the com-

King Boris III, who came to the Bulgarian throne in 1919.

munist countries in 1949. In that year Georgi Dimitrov died. He had been popular with the people and he was mourned throughout the country. His body was embalmed and placed in a mausoleum in the center of Sofia that was built in a matter of days. To this day, Bulgarians flock to see the mausoleum. They place flowers at its entrance and line up to see the embalmed body of their former leader.

Bulgaria joined the Warsaw Pact (a military alliance led by the Soviet Union) in 1954. Bulgaria became one of the Soviet Union's most faithful allies. The Bulgarian people admired the Soviets and put up impressive monuments in honor of the Soviet Army in many of their cities. They also erected statues and busts of Lenin, founder of the Soviet Union, and many streets and squares were named after Soviet heroes.

When the communist government of Bulgaria came to power, it decided to retain the country's traditional flag–a tricolor of white, green and red horizontal stripes. In the left-hand corner, the flag had a new coat of arms consisting of sheaves of corn with a lion in the middle topped by a red star. The base of the coat of arms was inscribed with the dates 861 and 1944. These represented the year the Bulgarians settled in their new land and the year they were liberated by the Soviet Army. A new anthem was also adopted which started with the words: "Dear Bulgaria, Land of Heroes."

The communist government banned all political opposition. Free speech and travel abroad were also banned. Bulgaria had only a few national newspapers and reviews, all of which represented the government's point of view. Books, films, plays and videos were strictly censored. Although the official Orthodox Church was allowed to function, many monasteries and churches were turned into museums. Many mosques where the Turkish minority worshipped were shut.

The communist leader, Todor Zhivkov, came to power in 1954 and the country prospered under his rule. Bulgaria had contacts with both eastern and western bloc countries. Thousands upon thousands of tourists from both east and west came to Bulgaria's Black Sea beaches and mountain resorts.

When economic reforms were introduced in Czechoslovakia in 1968, the leaders of the Soviet Union, Hungary, East Germany, Poland, and Bulgaria met in Warsaw and from there sent a joint ultimatum to Czechoslovakia to give up these reforms. As no satisfactory answer was given to the ultimatum, during the morning of August 21, 1969, Czechoslovakia was invaded by troops and tanks from Poland, the Soviet Union, and Hungary. Bulgaria, too, took part in the invasion with an army unit and this is the only occasion, since the end of the Second World War, when Bulgarian troops have invaded a foreign country.

The communist era in Bulgaria ended in 1989 with the overthrow of Todor Zhivkov, who had led Bulgaria since 1954. Political and economic upheaval followed with various governments trying to build a democracy and start a free-market economy. The people of Bulgaria were again allowed to practice their Catholic religion and many old traditions surfaced again. The government changed hands seven times during this time. By the winter of 1997 the people of Bulgaria were suffering. There was a great deal of corruption in the government, terrible inflation, large-scale unemployment, with long bread lines filled with starving people. The road to democracy had not been the easy one many people had hoped for and the people of Bulgaria finally rebelled in the streets and surrounded the parliament building demanding new elections. For over a month strikes and protests paralyzed the country until finally the new election was granted. The new government now has the task of rebuilding the country and its economy, a daunting and ongoing process.

7

Industry and
Transportation

Half a century ago, Bulgaria was a land of villages and small towns set in sheltered valleys among wooded mountains. The country, poor in minerals, had only a few iron foundries and food processing factories. There were also great difficulties in access and communication throughout the country. Most Bulgarians were peasants, some of whom worked for big landowners. Since then Bulgaria has become an industrial country with more than half the population working in industry. Today Bulgarian machinery, manufactured goods and farm produce are exported all over Europe.

The Second World War brought stagnation to industry and transportation in Bulgaria. After the war, the government decided to rebuild factories, roads and railway lines. Economic plans were drawn up by experts in Sofia. They were helped by economic aid from the then Soviet Union and other communist countries. Five Year Plans were adopted for the country's economic development.

The first Five Year Plan, which lasted from 1949 to 1953, laid the basis of modern Bulgarian industry. The fourth Five Year Plan (1961-1965) laid emphasis on heavy industry. The sixth Five Year Plan (1971-1975) set targets for doubling the output of the engineering and chemical industries. Bulgaria began producing trucks, cranes, electronic calculators and automation systems. Shipyards on the country's Black Sea coast produced 100,000-ton tankers.

Following the lead of other East European countries, Bulgarian firms were allowed to partner western firms in developing the country's newest industry—tourism. The Japanese, for instance, built a deluxe hotel in Sofia complete with a Japanese restaurant and garden.

The early building of new power stations was the key to the development of Bulgarian industry. The country could not rely on oil as a cheap source of power, so hydroelectric power stations were built near rivers in the mountains. High-tension cables across bleak mountains linked these stations with towns and factories in the plains. Bulgaria's first nuclear power station was built at Kozloduy in the northwest of the country and started to function in 1974, producing 1,760,000 kilowatts of electricity.

Most of Bulgaria's industry is concentrated in and around Sofia, in the middle of the country and on the Black Sea coast. In the north and northeast, farming still predominates.

Sofia has chemical and textile factories, light engineering works and industries specializing in processing food, mainly fruit and vegetables. Electrical and electronic goods are made there, as well as porcelain and glassware. Iron and steel mills are located at nearby Pernik. Plentiful supplies of water and electric power have stimulated the growth of new industries on the outskirts of the city.

Bulgaria's second largest city, Plovdiv, is in the middle of the country and is linked to Sofia by an international highway. Plovdiv is a fast-growing industrial, cultural, and intellectual center. It has engineering factories making spare parts for trucks, as well as cement factories and flour mills. Plovdiv has many enterprises which trade in local fruit and vegetables, wines, and tobacco.

Varna, Bulgaria's third largest city, is a Black Sea port. It is an important shipbuilding center, with dry docks and a ship repair plant. There are also factories making diesel engines and electrical appliances, textile mills, breweries, and food processing plants.

South of Varna is the Black Sea port of Burgas. Burgas is an industrial city with chemical plants and oil refineries. Bulgaria's second largest port, Burgas is the home port of the ocean fishing fleet and has numerous fish canneries. Huge ships anchor in its ports.

The biggest Bulgarian port on the Danube is Ruse. It is a modern town and major industrial center for producing farm machinery, plastics and insulation materials. There is also a shipyard on the banks of the Danube. The land around Ruse produces sugar beet which is processed at the local sugar beet factory.

Stara Zagora is one of Bulgaria's smaller towns but has good lines of communication with all parts of the Thracian Plain. It has

A robot used in the manufacture of electric motors. In recent years, great emphasis has been placed on developing Bulgarian industry.

a large factory making nitrogen-based fertilizers. There is also a cigarette factory, a brewery and a factory for making prefabricated houses.

The first railway in Bulgaria was opened in 1866. It linked Varna to Ruse, thus connecting the important Black Sea port with western Europe via the Danube. Today there are over 3,700 miles (6,000 kilometers) of railway track in Bulgaria and the main lines have been electrified. Sofia lies on the old route of the Orient

Express, which then continued its journey eastward as far as Istanbul.

There are more than 19,000 miles (over 31,000 kilometers) of main and secondary roads, of which 1,524 miles(2,453 kilometers) are connecting roads used by international traffic. The roads in the mountains have many hair-pin bends, but those in the plains are straight, lined with poplars, birch, and horse-chestnut trees giving shade from the fierce summer sun. These trees have their trunks whitewashed to protect them from ants.

Bulgaria lies on the main transportation routes from Belgrade in Yugoslavia to Istanbul in Turkey, and from Athens in Greece to Bucharest in Romania. People drive on the right-hand side of the road and there is a speed limit for cars of twenty-five miles (forty kilometers) an hour in built-up areas. Buses and coaches are popular forms of transportation. Many of the articulated red buses seen in Bulgarian towns are Ikarus buses imported from Hungary. They are almost twice as long as an ordinary bus and have three sets of wheels. The Chavdar coaches are used for inter-city travel, which is a cheap form of transportation. Bus and coach tickets are usually bought at the bus station and the passengers punch the tickets themselves in a small box fitted inside the vehicle.

Bulgaria also has a river fleet, which is used on the Danube. There is a passenger boat service for trips up and down the Danube from the port of Ruse. In addition, Bulgaria has an ocean-going fleet of forty ships which carry Bulgaria's trade to ports in the Black Sea, Mediterranean and Atlantic.

The country's airline is Balkanair and it operates from the three international airports at Sofia, Varna, and Burgas. Easy transportation to and from Bulgaria has stimulated the tourist industry. Tourists come from such countries as Finland, Russia, Poland, Britain, Ireland, and Germany.

8

Forests and Fisheries

In spite of many trees having been cut down for industry, building and firewood, 35 percent of the total area of Bulgaria is still covered with forests. Leaf-bearing trees such as birch, oak and alder account for three quarters of all trees, while firs and pines account for one quarter. Because so many trees were cut down in the past, a campaign was launched in 1945 to plant new forests. That campaign lasted 20 years and the country is still reaping the benefits of all the trees planted during that time. Young trees are still planted from nurseries to replace the timber which has been taken away. Tree nurseries grow thousands of beech and oak, firs and pines, which are then transplanted in the autumn and even exported to countries in need of their own forests.

There are natural coniferous forests in the Balkan and Rhodope Mountains. Fir trees can reach a height of over 80 feet (25 meters) and the trunks are as thick as a barrel. Lower down the mountain slopes, there are extensive forests of beech and ash mixed with

Wooden dolls for sale in a tourist shop.

hazel and maple. Acacia, willows, and poplars grow well in the warmer valleys.

Much of the timber is used for firewood, since Bulgaria is not rich in coal. Houses have terracotta or wood-burning stoves, and some of the chalets in the mountains have open hearths where a bright fire burns even on summer evenings when the wind blows from the mountain top. Beech and ash are used for making furniture, while oak is used for making barrels for the wine trade. Soft timber is used for building chalets and shelters high up in the mountains. Bulgarian wood-workers are skilled at making skis and toboggans for the tourist trade. Craftsmen also make wooden dolls and toys which are bought as souvenirs.

Lumbermen wearing steel helmets cut thousands of fir trees each year. The trees are cut into long logs, chained together, and then pulled down the mountain slope by a tractor. This is dangerous work because the tracks are steep and the tractors often have to negotiate deep ruts and boulders. Finally the logs are loaded onto heavy lorries and taken to the sawmills to be cut into planks of varying sizes.

Bulgarian woodmen are great experts at making flutes and whistles out of wood which they decorate with intricate designs. They also make tin bells (with bits of bent wire for clappers) for sheep which they sell to shepherds making their way to alpine pastures.

Fishing is an important industry in Bulgaria. Freshwater fishing takes place in the Danube and its tributaries. The catches include perch, pike and catfish. The fishermen send most of their catches to the ports of Ruse and Silistra where the fish is smoked or salt-ed and packed into barrels. The most famous fish of the Danube are the sterlet and sturgeon, from whose roe black caviar is pre-pared and put into small china pots. Danube caviar is a luxury to be found in expensive restaurants and wealthy houses in London, Paris and elsewhere. Carp is bred in lakes and fish ponds while rainbow trout is caught in mountain streams. Some Bulgarian restaurants specialize in fish dishes and one can always tell them by the sign of a fish at their entrance.

Deep-sea fishing is done by smacks and trawlers which go to the Black Sea and Atlantic Ocean. They catch sardines, herrings, mackerel, turbot, grey mullet, tuna and cod. Some of the fish caught in the Atlantic is processed on the spot by factory ships.

Burgas is the headquarters of the Bulgarian fishing fleet. It has repair yards for fishing boats and nets, a big cannery and a Fish Research Institute.

9

Farms and Crops

Despite industrial development and fast-growing towns, about half of Bulgaria's population are still employed in farming. The country produces enough food for home consumption and for the many tourists who visit the resorts each year. There is also a surplus for export to western Europe. Farms also supply manufacturing industry with raw materials such as sugar, oil of roses, and fruit and vegetables for canning.

After the Second World War, the government decided to set up cooperative farms by amalgamating peasant small holdings. Very few peasants liked the idea of working on a cooperative farm and the government had to use force. By 1958, about 3,300 cooperative farms had been set up with an average size of 2,965 acres (1,200 hectares). During the next twelve years, these farms tripled the amount of stock and machinery they owned, became more productive and raised the wages of the peasants.

The government then decided to establish about 160 very large cooperative farms which were over twenty times the size of the

Watering crops on a Bulgarian farm.

average farm. This system made it possible for the farms to build canneries and meat-processing plants for their own products. Drainage and irrigation also improved the value of land and the quality of crops. Factories at Vratsa, Dimitrovgrad, and Stara Zagora produce large quantities of chemical fertilizers for use on farms. After 1991, the farmland was redistribute from heavy state farms and returned to private ownership.

Bulgaria is a major producer of wheat and corn. Wheat is an important crop because it provides the staple food for the population. The mills grind the wheat into flour which is used for making the standard white bread, rolls and crisp rings (like German *pretzels*) which are strung on sticks or string and sold in most cafés. The corn is used for feeding to poultry and pigs and for making starch, glucose, and alcohol. The dried leaves and stems of the corn plant are used as fodder for cattle and sheep in winter. Bulgaria also produces large quantities of barley, oats, sunflowers, sugar beet and potatoes. The oats grow well in the hills and valleys.

The Kazanluk valley, also known as the Valley of the Roses, lies on the main road between Sofia and Burgas. It is unique in Europe and has been famous for its rose gardens since the 17th century. The best perfumes in Europe are made from the petals of roses. The rose-pickers set out with large wicker baskets to pick the flowers early in the morning before the dew has been lifted off the petals, and they send them straight to the perfume distillery. One gram of oil (or attar) of roses is produced from two thousand petals. This oil is worth its weight in gold. Today, Bulgaria is the world's largest exporter of the oil of roses.

Rose research workers in Kazanluk are now working on better ways of extracting the oil from the petals. Two hundred and fifty oil-bearing types of roses are grown in experimental gardens owned by the Bulgarian Rose Corporation. Roses are also used for making rose petal jam which is eaten from small china plates no larger than coffee saucers; and the flowers are used for making a rose brandy, pink in color and very sweet.

The hot summers and plentiful supply of irrigation water in the

Thracian Plain make the area suitable for growing tobacco and rice. The farms growing tobacco sell their crop to the large tobacco factory in Dimitrovo for making cigarettes and cigars. The hills and fertile valleys bordering on the Thracian Plain are covered with plum and apple orchards. The plum orchards produce extremely sweet plums which are dried in special ovens and then exported as prunes. Much of the plum crop is put to ferment in vats, and then distilled and turned into a strong brandy called *slivova*. If the brandy is distilled twice, it is even stronger and then called *palinka*.

In the extreme south of Bulgaria, there are small citrus plantations where oranges and lemons are grown. The rind of the lemon is used for making an oil essence and the popular candied lemon peel. There are fig trees and mulberry groves in sheltered valleys.

Tobacco drying. Tobacco is an important crop on the Thracian plain.

The black and white mulberries are used for making jam or wine. The leaves of the mulberry tree are fed to silk worms from whose cocoons natural silk is extracted. Much of the silk is used for making traditional costumes.

Bulgarian market gardeners grow a wide variety of vegetables. They grow gherkins (small cucumbers) and green and red peppers for pickling in vinegar and water. They also grow large numbers of tomatoes, eggplants, beans and chilies which are used for flavoring stews and other dishes. Some farms specialize in growing herbs like thyme, rosemary and parsley and medicinal flowers like camomile and lime-tree blossom which are used for making herbal mixtures. There are chemist shops in Bulgaria which sell only herbal teas for stomach upsets and various natural powders from big stone jars.

The foothills of the Balkan and Rhodope Mountains have sunny slopes and good soil for vine-growing. The vines are trained on a trellis and carefully pruned and sprayed in early spring. The grape-picking season starts in August when the fruit is eaten fresh. The late-ripening grapes are used for making Bulgarian red and white wines which are exported to many other countries. The grape skins and stalks, left over after the wine is pressed, are left to ferment and then distilled into five- or three-star brandies.

Bees have been kept in Bulgaria since Thracian times. The visitor can see today rows upon rows of blue-painted bee hives in the hills near acacia groves. The beekeepers supply honey for shops and the tourist trade and wax for candles, polish and tanning. The special honey made by the bees for rearing queens called royal jelly is also used as a medicinal product.

Bulgaria is a land of sheep; there are around 10 million in the country. Since the land is unfenced, flocks are watched over by shepherds. They can be seen on the lower slopes of mountains with watchful dogs and patient donkeys wearing ornamental saddles. The sheep are bred for meat and wool, and their milk is used for the white cheese which is so popular in Bulgaria. The peasants and cooperative farms also raise two and a half million pigs, as well as somewhere between one and two million cattle. There are thousands of goats in the far south, and occasionally working oxen can still be seen.

Horse breeding is carried out at Shumen in eastern Bulgaria, in

Medicinal herbs on sale in a street market in Sofia.

A vineyard in the foothills of the Balkan Mountains.

the Danube plain and near the town of Balĉik in the Dobrudja plain. There are several breeds of horses in Bulgaria; the best known is the East Bulgarian, a well developed and compact animal of around sixteen hands. On the land the working horse is still much in evidence and there are horses in towns too, as well as pack ponies carrying provisions to mountain farmhouses and to the cafés and shelters provided for skiers, walkers and mountaineers. There are also equestrian centers with a variety of horses including thoroughbreds and Anglo-Arabs.

10

Village Life

In order to see what life is like in the mountains of Bulgaria, let's visit a village in the southwestern corner of the country. The village is called Deravna and is situated on a main road passing through a narrow valley. All around are the bleak, grey peaks of the Rila Mountains. Lower down the mountain sides, there are thick forests of firs mixed with beech and oak. The village is approached by a winding cobbled road. On the right-hand side, a fast stream rushes over big boulders in a bed of hard granite rock. On the edge of the village there is a stone monument in memory of Bulgarian patriots who died fighting the Turks over a century ago for the independence of their country. According to legend, the village was founded by a young couple who fled from the invading Turks and hid in a nearby cave.

A big sign with the word Deravna marks the village boundary. The houses of the village are solidly built. They are made of brick, plastered and painted in yellow or ochre. The roofs are square, with broad eaves, and covered in red pantiles. Most houses have one story and a wooden balcony from which washing flutters in the wind. Round each house there is a high stone wall and a heavy iron gate. A cherry tree grows in the small front garden and there are creeping vines all round.

Inside, the houses have carved wooden ceilings and are furnished with low tables and chairs with intricate patterns. Red and blue locally-made carpets and rugs cover the floors and walls. In the dining-room, there is usually a dresser covered with colored plates and wood carvings.

It is summer and the village street is full of peasants dressed in drab working clothes preparing to go to their fields. Several horse-drawn carts are being loaded with tools and bags. As the peasants are about to leave, the sky suddenly grows dark, and one of the violent thunderstorms, which are quite common in the mountains, breaks out. The rain comes pelting down, and everyone in the village struggles to keep the drenching water from flooding the carts. Then the storm ends as suddenly as it had started, and the sun comes out, making the grey cobblestones and pantiles sparkle and filling the air with warmth.

Further down the road, a small market is full of people and stalls. Some of the stalls sell vegetables, heaps of potatoes and green beans, onions and cucumbers. There are also boxes of cherries and raspberries for sale. One stall sells pots and pans, earthenware plates and bowls, chains and plastic buckets.

In the evening, a minibus arrives in the village with a group of tourists who are invited to dinner by an old peasant woman famous for her cooking. She welcomes her guests on the doorstep with bread, salt and herbs as is the Bulgarian custom. When the

Picking lavender by hand. Although great progress has been made, much farmwork is still done by traditional methods in Bulgaria.

guests are seated at the table in the dining room, a young girl appears carrying a bottle of home-made plum brandy and small glasses. After toasting each other, the guests begin their dinner with a plate of cold cucumber soup followed by a salad of tomatoes and cucumber sprinkled with cream cheese. This is followed by pork stew, homemade rolls, and red wine. The dinner ends with cakes and fruit. The guests are also entertained by two village musicians who play the guitar and sing folk songs as old as the hills.

Sofia and Other Cities

Sofia, the capital of Bulgaria, lies in the center of a high plain, 1,739 feet (530 meters) above sea level, surrounded by the Balkan and Central Mountains and Mount Vitosha which dominates its skyline. There was a settlement here in prehistoric times; and early in its 8,000-year history it became a meeting point of busy trade routes.

Excavations have shown that Sofia is one of the most ancient cities of Europe. Philip of Macedon took the city in 339 B.C. In the first century B.C., the Thracian tribe of Serdi settled here calling the settlement Serdica. During the Roman period in the first century A.D., Emperor Trajan fortified Serdica and called it Ulpia Serdica. After the Romans withdrew, the Huns, led by their cruel chieftain Attila, ravaged the place killing many people. In the sixth century A.D. under the reign of Emperor Justinian I of Byzantium, Serdica was rebuilt and surrounded by thick walls and towers. In the early ninth century of the Christian era, the Bulgarian armies under Khan Kroum captured the city and called it Sredets, which

A view over Sofia, Bulgaria's capital.

means "The Center." The name Sofia appeared for the first time in its long history only in 1376 when the Bulgarian tsar Ivan Shishman gave the city and the surrounding land by charter to the local monastery. The invading Turks finally captured Sofia in 1386 and made it the administrative center for their European provinces.

Sofia has the motto "Ever growing, never old" on its coat of arms. As more and more Bulgarians settled in Sofia, the city expanded and grew in all directions. Because of its wide boulevards, beautiful gardens and monuments, Sofia has the reputation of being a very clean and green city. Today, it has flourishing industries and a population of over 1,100,000. It is not only a place of historical interest but also the center of Bulgaria's administrative and cultural life. The prime minister and other ministers have their offices there. The Bulgarian National Assembly holds its meetings in the Parliament Building in the city's center.

Perhaps one of Sofia's most striking features is the variety of historical buildings and monuments in the city's center. The Alexander Nevski Memorial Church has twelve gilt domes. Inside the church has marble floors, huge chandeliers and many frescoes of saints on which thirty-two painters worked. Not far away is the red brick rotunda (round building with a dome) of St. George still

The domes of the Alexander Nevski Memorial Church.

The magnificent interior of the Alexander Nevski Memorial Church.

standing among ruins from Roman times. Unique in Eastern Europe is the Monument of the Liberators, an equestrian statue of Tsar Alexander II of Russia and his officers, in one of Sofia's finest squares. The streets all around the square are paved with yellow cobblestones and there is hardly any traffic.

Then there is the Russian Church of St. Nicholas, also with gilt domes and a green roof, and the Church of St. Sofia which was built in the sixth century A.D. Nearby is the Tomb of the Unknown Warrior with its constantly burning flame. Next to it is a big lion in bronze looking on at the passersby.

Prior to the overthrow of communism, Sofia's Georgi Dimitrov Mausoleum, built in 1949, contained the embalmed body of Georgi Dimitrov, who was Bulgarian Prime Minister from 1946 to 1949. Long lines of Bulgarian people with bunches of flowers could be seen outside the mausoleum every day waiting to pay their respects to their former leader. In 1990, Dimitrov's body was removed and buried in the central cemetery and there is talk of destroying the mausoleum.

A chemist's shop in Sofia, selling traditional herbal remedies.

Sofia has wide roads and boulevards lined with trees along which traffic flows in a steady stream. The city has cream and red buses as well as yellow trolleys which deliver their passengers outside open-air cafés, superstores and office buildings.

Sofia has an Academy of Sciences, a University and a National Theater. The National Art Gallery was formerly the King's Palace while the National Palace of Culture is a modern building made of steel and glass.

Because it is so centrally placed, Sofia is Bulgaria's center for railways and long-distance coaches. The city has a good market in which the farms can sell their produce. In exchange, the farmers buy clothes and hardware and all sorts of consumer goods.

Fountains outside the ultra-modern National Palace of Culture.

The impressive National Theatre building in Sofia, the center of Bulgaria's cultural and artistic life.

About 37 miles(60 kilometers) southeast on the main road from Sofia is the small market town of Samokov. With a population of 30,000, Samokov lies on the banks of the Black Iskar in the foothills of the Rila Mountains. The river had been dammed further down stream to provide water for drinking and for the factories of Sofia. The town has a mosque, a church and a synagogue. It also has the bronze statue of a wild goat and an ornamental fountain in the town square. The former king used to spend his holidays here in the local palace which has now been turned into a rest house. The road eastward from Samokov is full of bends as

71

The mosque in Samokov—a reminder that the Turkish Muslim influence is still quite strong in Bulgaria.

it descends from the hills into the Thracian Plain. Then the road straightens out and is bordered by leafy trees. The countryside is green with tobacco and maize plantations. On the right, the skyline is formed by the peaks and valleys of the Rhodope Mountains. The road leads to the ancient city of Plovdiv, situated

A general view of new Plovdiv, Bulgaria's second largest city.

on three hills on the banks of the Maritsa River, some 79 miles (128 kilometers) from Sofia.

Plovdiv is Bulgaria's second largest city with a population of 357,000. It was founded over five thousand years ago and the settlement was originally called Eumolpias. Philip II of Macedon conquered Eumolpias and changed its name to Philippopolis. In their turn, the Romans called it Trimontium or the City on Three Hills. Plovdiv acquired its present name only in the 18th century when it had already become a large and thriving city. Plovdiv is an important industrial and trading center. Part of Plovdiv is modern and part is ancient, with narrow cobbled streets and houses

73

Part of the old city of Plovdiv, with its narrow cobbled streets.

with bay windows and arches. There is a tunnel under one of the hills to allow the traffic to move freely from one side of the town to the other. The center of Plovdiv is also the shopping area and is enclosed for pedestrians only. Near by there is a large amphitheater of white stone dating from Roman times which is still used for open-air shows. Plovdiv has several mosques and churches.

The countryside around Plovdiv is full of orchards and market

74

gardens. There are also long greenhouses for the production of early vegetables in spring, especially tomatoes and cucumbers, green peppers and eggplants.

Stara Zagora is another town in the Thracian Plain, some 43 miles (70 kilometers) northeast of Plovdiv. In Roman times, the place was a fortress called Augusta Trajana. Today, Stara Zagora is an important transportation junction and industrial town with a population of 156,000. It has a theater, an art gallery and several research institutes. There is also a monument in memory of those who fell in the Russo-Turkish war of 1877. Recently a Roman amphitheater was excavated in the town center. The countryside around has tobacco plantations and vineyards.

Varna is Bulgaria's third largest city with a population of 305,000. It is situated at the head of Varna Bay on the Black Sea coast some 300 miles (470 kilometers) from Sofia. The city was founded in the fourth century B.C. by Greek traders who called their colony Odessos. During the reign of Tsar Ivan Assen II, Varna was a busy port trading with Constantinople, the Italian cities of Genoa and Venice, and Dubrovnik in Yugoslavia. The Turks conquered the city in 1391. Varna played an important role during the Crimean War from 1853 to 1856 when it was used as a base by the British and French armies who at that time were fighting the Russians on the side of the Turks.

Today Varna is a busy industrial and commercial center. It is also a seaside resort, with tourists from many countries staying at modern hotels. The beautiful cathedral with its many domes and crosses is in the center of the city. Varna has several museums and

The Pobiti Kamani rock formations between Shumen and Varna.

the ruins of Roman baths. Its boulevards are lined with plane trees, while in the middle there are flower beds. Underground subways with small shops connect the wide pavements on either side of the boulevards.

Varna has a college for training sailors and seamen, and open-air festivals are held there during the summer months. Two-lane highways north and south of the city connect it to the many seaside resorts along the wooded coastline.

Some 93 miles (150 kilometers) to the south of Varna, across the long bridge spanning the bay and the eastern tip of the Balkan

Mountains, is Burgas, Bulgaria's second largest port on the Black Sea. A century ago, Burgas was a fishing village but today it has factories and flour mills. Many of the inhabitants are also employed in the tourist industry and fish canning. Burgas is the chief port for the export of southeastern Bulgaria's farm produce and has a population of 187,000.

The city has a modern look with wide boulevards and new public buildings. It has a theater, picture gallery and research institutes. Burgas Baths just outside the city use water from mineral springs.

Ruse, in northern Bulgaria, is situated on the banks of the Danube. It was founded by the Romans who built a fortress here and called it Sexaginta Prista (the city of sixty ships). The modern town took shape under Turkish rule in the fifteenth century when it became a military center. The countryside around is rich in sugar beet fields and vineyards.

Today Ruse has a population of 190,000 and is an important river port and road and rail junction because of the bridges across the Danube. Ruse has a theater, several museums, an opera company and a symphony orchestra. The Monument to Freedom, guarded by stone lions, is always lit up at night in the central square.

12

Seaside Resorts and Spas

Wooded hills slope gently towards the sea in Bulgaria. There are also many beaches with fine yellow sand. The sea has no tides so the beaches stay clean and bear no water marks. Because of this, many resorts have been built along the coast between Varna and the Romanian border. This coastline is also known as the Bulgarian Riviera.

Zlatni Pjasâci (Golden Sands), a seaside resort, lies 10.5 miles (17 kilometers) north of Varna to which it is connected by a two-lane highway. The beach itself is 2.4 miles (4 kilometers) long and 328 feet (100 meters) wide in places. Many multi-storied hotels have been built among the woods on the hillside. There are also hotels along the seafront, with shops and cafés, mineral-spring medical centers, and sports and entertainment centers. The promenade is shaded by acacia and plane trees. A little further north along the coast is Albena, a 1970s-style resort. Albena, has long, wide beaches and is situated in a sheltered bay.

Across the bay from Albena can be seen the white cliffs of

Golden Sands, a resort on Bulgaria' Black Sea coast.

Balĉik which, before the Second World War, belonged to Romania. Balĉik lies on a hillside. It has steep cobbled roads and honeycomb pavements. The former palace of Queen Mary of Romania is just outside Balĉik by the seashore. The palace, with its minaret, is in the middle of a beautiful terraced garden with paths of crazy paving, tumbling creepers and honeysuckle and sunken rose gardens. There are a great variety of roses with different names— Montezuma, Brandenburg, Monte Carlo, Queen of Roses and many others. Huge ancient urns stand in corners and outside the summer house with its arches and columns. There is also a small chapel, no bigger than a hut, with frescoes on its walls. On one of the walls in the garden there is a metal plaque signed by Queen Mary thanking the architect Gaetan Denize for building such a

79

The white cliffs of Balĉik.

beautiful place. Queen Mary herself stated in her will that her heart should be cut out of her body and buried at Balĉik.

At the other end of the country, some 59 miles (95 kilometers) southwest of Sofia, is the Kiustendil Spa in the valley of the Struma River. The spa was known in Roman times when it was called Pautalia and it had a shrine dedicated to Asclepius, the patron god of medicine. Kiustendil has forty hot springs which are almost boiling at 256 degrees Fahrenheit (76 degrees Celsius). People suffering from rheumatism, arthritis and heart diseases go there because the steaming water is sulphurous. Kiustendil has a church dating from the 12th century and an art gallery. Roman ruins were unearthed here during recent excavations.

Some 45 miles (72 kilometers) south of Sofia is the resort of

A frozen fountain in Borovets.

Borovets at an altitude of 4,265 feet(1,300 meters) among the pine-covered slopes of the Rila Mountains. The air is very pure and clean, and people come to the resort for the treatment of lung diseases, bronchitis, diabetes and silicosis (caused by breathing quartz dust). Borovets has a small square with fountains, post office, cafés and shops selling souvenirs. Chalet-type hotels are scattered about the pine forests. In winter, Borovets is popular with skiers because it has excellent ski runs, a ski-jump and a slalom track. Hikers come and stay in Borovets in summer. They hire the chair lifts which take them to the top of the mountain from where they can walk among the bare rocks and stunted pines. Cafés and shelters provide refreshments all the year round.

81

13

Churches and Monasteries

The Bulgarian Tsar Boris I adopted Christianity in 865. He encouraged the saintly brothers Cyril and Methodius to preach the gospel to his people. In this way, the Bulgarians belonged to the Early Christian Church. When the Christian Church split into East and West in the eleventh century, the Bulgarians chose the Orthodox Eastern Church (orthodox means "true faith") whose head is still the Patriarch of Constantinople.

In the Middle Ages, Bulgarian tsars built magnificent churches and monasteries. Masons and carpenters, architects and artists were brought from Constantinople (modern-day Istanbul), Greece and Italy to build and decorate churches. The walls and ceilings of these churches, both inside and outside, were covered with bright frescoes which showed scenes from the life of Jesus Christ, the Virgin Mary and the Apostles. In keeping with eastern traditions, they built a wooden screen between the altar and the nave called an iconostasis. These screens consisted of icons (religious pictures)

The magnificent Rila Monastery.

showing the faces of saints painted in vivid colors and with golden haloes.

Many monasteries were also built in the mountains and sheltered valleys. Some had thick walls and towers to protect them from marauding Turks who hated Christians calling them "infidels." With the passage of time, the monasteries became places where people could learn to read and write. The monks were also great artists who taught their apprentices the art of wood carving, painting and making mosaics.

The communist regime had discouraged the practices and traditions of religion in the peoples' lives. After the fall of communism there was a renewed interest in these traditions and the Orthodox Church has been flourishing. The beautiful Rila Monastery is situated 75 miles (121 kilometers) from Sofia in a wooded valley of the Rila Mountains. The foundations of the monastery were laid in the mid-tenth century, but the monastery takes its name from Ivan Rilski, or John of Rils, who made his abode there. Soon the monastery became a center of Bulgarian culture and won the admiration of the Turkish sultans who gave it certain rights and privi-

A striking view of the inner courtyard at Rila Monastery, the foundations of which were laid in the 10th century.

Long a center of Bulgarian culture, Rila Monastery attracts thousands of visitors every year.

leges. The Turkish sultan, Mohammed II, for instance, gave the monastery a huge candle which has been preserved to this day.

The monastery is protected by thick walls and strong gates. The tall tower inside the monastery dates from 1335. But otherwise most of the monastery was rebuilt in the 19th century after a fire.

The monastery church has five domes and many frescoes both inside and outside its walls. Some of the frescoes show red devils with tridents tormenting the sinners who have gone to hell. Many of the paintings were done by Zahari Zograph, an 18th-century master painter.

The monastery was used as a national museum during the communist era, but was returned to the church following the 1991 reforms. It has a library and a collection of tapestries and vestments, gold and silver chalices and crosses. There is also an intricate wooden cross of oak which was boiled and then carved with a needle. It took the artist twenty-nine years to complete the work, by which time he was blind.

Bulgaria is also famous for her rock monasteries. Aladzha Monastery is near the Black Sea coast. It has cells hewn in the rock and a small church. The walls of the cells were once covered in paintings. The Ivanovo rock monastery dates from the twelfth century. It was hewn into rocks in a gorge of the Russenski Lom River. The hermits' cells and chapels have well preserved frescoes commissioned by Tsar Ivan Alexander in the 14th century.

Some Bulgarians and members of ethnic minorities such as the Turks are religious people who like to go to their local church or mosque to pray or attend divine services. These worshippers light wax candles and place them on stands inside the church; they make the sign of the cross and kiss icons, which are objects of worship. They participate in religious festivals and hold special services to remember the dead, where prayers are said, candles lit and cakes and fruit offered to be blessed in memory of those who have died.

14

Schools and Sports

Today there are three types of schools in Bulgaria—state, municipal, and private, including a number of religious schools. After the changes from communism in the early 1990s there was widespread reform. In 1991, the Law on Public Education was passed which states that "no political activity is allowed in the system of public education." This began the depolitization of Bulgaria's schools.

Under the new laws, boys and girls in towns and villages begin school at the age of six. Pupils have to stay at school until the age of sixteen. During these years they study general subjects such as mathematics, grammar, literature, nature study and music. After the age of 16 those who so wish can go to a technical school, to professional vocational school, or to general high schools. There are some religious high-schools available. Those who can pass the examinations go to a specialized school which has a more academic curriculum. Between the ages of 16 and 19 children can study

Bulgarian children at the Banner of Peace festival, held in 1985 to promote international cooperation and understanding.

foreign languages as well as Bulgarian literature, history, geography and mathematics.

The Academy of Sciences is the highest institution for scientific research in Bulgaria. It supervises the work of 200 research institutes and there are nearly 8,000 research workers in the country. In 1990 a new education law on academic freedom was passed which gave individual institutions of higher education independence to administer their own curriculums without government interference. The changes in the Bulgarian educational system are

88

on-going as help from Western countries brings more professors, and more students to study in Bulgaria's schools.

All schoolchildren enjoy long summer holidays which begin in June and end in mid-September. Bulgaria has long and warm summers. This means that young people can spend much of their vacations on the Black Sea coast. Many of the resorts have large swimming pools in which lanes are marked out for competitions. Boys and girls can also go swimming in rivers and lakes or fish for trout and pike.

Bulgaria's mountain slopes and snowy winters mean that young people can practice skiing and tobogganing for several months in the year. Gondola- and chair-lifts as well as chalets and cabins

Fishing in the Struma River.

have been built for skiers at many resorts in the Rila and Balkan Mountains. People living in the plains can skate on frozen ponds or open-air ice rinks.

Physical training is popular with all ages in Bulgaria. Over three million people take part each year in the national games called Spartakiades. Athletes have excelled in wrestling, weight lifting, basketball, and volleyball.

15

Arts and Festivals

The Bulgarian people have a rich tradition of folklore—beliefs, customs and legends—which has its roots in the distant past. Much of this folklore came from Thracian, Roman and Greek history represented by tombs, sculptures, pottery and gold and silver treasures found near Varna and going back five thousand years. Tools, pottery of all sorts, carpets and clothes made by craftsmen are often decorated with shapes and pictures seen on old vases and ornaments. The wall paintings and carvings in palaces and churches, which date from the Middle Ages, were carried out by Byzantine artists and so influenced the work of later Bulgarian painters and carvers.

The original music and dancing of the Bulgarian people consisted of songs and movements based on happenings in everyday life. Religious chants which were developed in the 13th and 14th centuries were handed down from generation to generation. Today, singers and dancers wear colorful national costumes and often perform on radio and television. Bulgarians are also good

Bulgarian folk dancers in traditional costume.

opera singers and some are world-famous. Professional musicians play violins and flutes or guitars and are often seen in cafes or at private parties. There are also amateur groups in towns and villages who carry out performances of folk music. Some of these groups win prizes at international competitions and festivals.

Bulgarian craftsmen are famous for the dolls they make, many of which are bought by tourists as souvenirs. Some of the dolls are made of hair and rags and dressed in miniature national costumes. Others are made of wood, are hollow inside and contain a bottle of perfume.

Bulgarian folk art—songs, dances and costumes—is kept alive at national festivals and international competitions. A competition of folk songs and dances is held every year in the first half of August at Burgas. There are also traditional Music Weeks in Sofia and Ruse. Every year in June there is an International Competition of Bulgarian Pop Music held on the Black Sea coast. An International Festival of Chamber Music is held annually in Plovdiv. The Festival of Roses is celebrated at the beginning of June in the Valley of Roses when the rose-picking season normally starts.

16

How the Country is Run

After King Simeon was deposed in 1946, Bulgaria was called a People's Republic. A constitution was adopted in 1947, but this was replaced by a new constitution in 1971 after a referendum was held throughout the country.

The 1971 constitution proclaimed Bulgaria a socialist state led by the Communist Party. All citizens over 18 years of age could vote and be elected. All industry, transportation, and natural resources belonged to the state but ordinary citizens could own their houses and cars.

After the overthrow of communism a new constitution was established in July 1991. This constitution gave the Bulgarian people all the power in the country through their elected governmental bodies. Bulgaria was made a republic keeping the parliamentary form of government.

The Bulgarian parliament is known as the National Assembly and has 400 seats. The constitution states that the National Assembly represents the will of the people and their sovereignty.

Its members are elected for a term of four years and they decide how the country is to be governed. The Assembly passes laws and fixes taxes. The Council of Ministers, the executive body of the government, along with the president, decides when war shall be declared and peace made. The president appoints Bulgaria's ambassadors to foreign countries and meets the ambassadors of other countries who come to Bulgaria. The president is elected every five years by popular vote.

Bulgaria is now divided into nine provinces called *oblasti*. The provinces are divided into communities (*obshtini*). Local elections are held in these communities and the people can vote for their local officials and on referendums.

All Bulgarian citizens are equal before the law and they enjoy no privileges based on race, sex, religion or education. Anybody who stirs up racial or religious hatred is punished by the law. Women enjoy equal rights with men and that includes equal pay for equal work. All male citizens are compelled to do military service.

Bulgaria has two national television stations and two privately-owned channels. There are many radio programs available, both privately owned and foreign.

Bulgaria had a national insurance plan but in 1990 state control was removed. Pensions are paid to men and women according to the length of service. Bulgaria was the first country in the world to pay pensions to farm workers. Parents receive family allowances for their children.

Bulgaria is an active member of the United Nations

СЪЕДИНЕНИЕТО ПРАВИ СИЛАТА

The National Assembly building in Sofia.

Organization and takes part in the proceedings of the United Nations General Assembly and other United Nations bodies. Bulgarian delegates to the United Nations in the past usually followed the lead given by the Soviet Union but now Bulgaria is an independent republic on its own.

17

Bulgaria in the World Today

We have learned about Bulgaria's new industries and growing towns, her vast forests and productive farms, her new struggle toward a democratic society. We have seen that the tourist trade is starting to bring the country much-needed foreign currency. Yet the Bulgarians still have low wages and few cars compared with people living in Western Europe. Shops are not full of goods and some of them are of poor quality. Bulgaria is a developing country in need of more cars and machinery, and hard currency from abroad such as dollars and pounds. In order to earn this money, Bulgaria sells much of its farm produce, tobacco, and wines abroad. The government is trying to find new markets where it can sell timber and the manufactured goods which the country produces.

Bulgaria's beautiful mountains and beaches on the Black Sea have attracted many tourists in recent years. This is because the government has built new hotels and provided first-class services such as restaurants with good food and cheap travel by coach and air. Passport and customs formalities have been reduced to encourage people to visit the country.

Housing in towns is still a problem in Bulgaria. Peasants have come from the countryside and settled in towns to work in the factories. Housing estates have been built, but there is still a shortage of apartments and various public services.

There are nearly three million workers in Bulgaria who belong to industrial and white-collar trade-unions.

In foreign policy, the present Bulgarian government believes in friendship and cooperation with countries of both the East and West. Bulgaria gives some economic help to the developing countries in Asia and Africa and accepts students from those countries for training in colleges and industry.

Things are changing fast in modern Bulgaria. After the Second World War, Bulgaria was one of the poorest countries in Eastern Europe. The standard of living of the Bulgarian people increased for a number of years. Economic growth slowed down in 1991 because of the restructuring of the economy to a free-market system.

The Bulgarian government pursues a policy of peace with all its neighbors. Bulgaria is gradually making economic progress as it works toward free enterprise. The Bulgarian people have lived through many dangers throughout their long history. Though they still live at the crossroads of the Balkans, where East meets West, they feel confident that peace and democracy has at last come to stay in their part of the world.

GLOSSARY

cudgel	Short heavy club
Cyrillic alphabet	Alphabet used in some parts of eastern Europe and Asia invented by St. Cyril in the 9th century
fresco	Painting done on freshly spread moist plaster with water-based paints that seap into the plaster and dry there
hydroelectric power	Electricity produced by waterpower
Ottoman Empire	Turkish kingdom that dominated southeastern Europe, western Asia, and north Africa from the 14th to 19th centuries
oblasti	Provinces in Bulgaria
roe	Fish eggs sold as a delicacy called caviar
slivova	Brandy made of distilled plums
tsar	Variation of the word czar, it refers to emperors, usually in parts of eastern Europe
Warsaw Pact	Military alliance of countries in Eastern Europe led by the Soviet Union

INDEX

101